DATE DUE

B · 1 2010

Also by Rob Smith:

Novels:
> *Night Voices* (2006)
> *Children of Light* (2006)

Short Story Collection:
> *McGowan's Call* (2007)

Nonfiction:
> *Cultural Perspectives on the Bible: A Beginner's Guide* (2007)

Literary Criticism:
> *Hogwarts, Narnia, and Middle Earth: Places Upon a Time* (2007)

256 Zones of Gray

Rob Smith

BIRD DOG PUBLISHING

HURON, OHIO

Bird Dog Press
A Division of Bottom Dog Press
PO Box 425 / Huron, OH 44839
http://members.aol.com/Lsmithdog/bottomdog
A Member of IMPAAC
Independent Midwest Publishers And Authors Consortium
www.impaac-online.org

Cover Photo by Rob Smith©
Layout and Design by Susanna Sharp-Schwacke

Acknowledgements:

"Catbird" won the 2006 Robert Frost Poetry Award and was
published online (www.frostfoundation.org).
"17 December 1903" was published online in the virtual
chapbook *First Flights* (2003) (www.thewritegallery.com).

Bird Dog Publishing

Huron, Ohio

Dedication:

For Nancy,
Leslie, Adam, and Jeff

Contents:

Patterns

Love

Reflections

Earth

256 Zones of Gray

Rain is an excuse
I didn't want to use so
I went out into
the filter of cloud,
a day imitating Ansel Adams with
256 zones of gray,
each a color of its own,
each distinct,
each alive,
and crisp,
and clear.
The autumn foliage
plots to cheat the day
with muted pigment,
but light doesn't allow it.
Water, sky, tree, grasses
full of color, yet not.
Silver water beads on waxy leaves.
I won't sit on the park bench today,
but stand at the juncture of black and white,
in the cast of muted light,
in the spectrum of filtered sky.

Catbird

I spit in the river like a boy,
but nobody saw me,
I made sure of that.
I was dry
after running across the field,
with lungs heaving
and mouth powdery.
It was like that, and I stopped
on the bridge to quench my thirst
by staring at the water.

So I spit.

It was white and chalky swirling
in black water 'till it caught the
current and was lost in the foam
over rocks and broken twigs.
I watched beyond what I saw,
and no one else saw or spoke except
a catbird on the railing.

Burial Ground

The really old cemeteries
forget themselves,
attracting only the living,
and not the dead.
In this field where no grass
has been uprooted
for seasons uncounted,
the departed already have,
and new generations refuse to gather.

Genealogists come,
but do not stay.
They read the stones
as if deciphering
glyphs of an ancient race
while sandstone defies
its carver by giving up letters.
Halloween brings the fearful,
afraid of the wrong things.
They come to the safety
of abandoned bodies
telling such tales of fright
that only living hands could accomplish,
hands present here no longer.

If a murderous fist
with axe and blade were here,
long time has passed since
malice crossed mind
or will drove the fatal strike.
Some cry out to leave them alone,
as though bothering them was in our power.
"Let the dead be!" they say.
"Be what?" I ask. "Dead?"
Is there some other form of substance
I could invoke upon them?
Happy?
Joyful?
Peaceful bliss?
Yes, the place has become peacefully empty,
but if there is more to give than words,
another arm than mine must do it.

Edge of Color

The teacher named it
Roy G. Biv.
I didn't know any Roys,
except Rogers,
and never any Bivs,
but this was hardly a stranger
to those who asked
for the hall light
left on
and the door
open a crack.
Visible light,
always a friend,
but having edges
not just in darkness now,
but at "R" and "V."

The school nurse would
take us in groups
down the hall to a
small room,
six at a time.
There, in the hushed silence
of a violet glow,
she'd run a hand
through our hair
looking for lice.
It was the color of light
on the edge of light,
wondrous thing,
beauty at the end of biv.
I want to return
to that room
and look again,
over the edge of color.

Washburn Ditch

There's a place where the ditch
cuts under the highway
and great pipes carry the flow,
channeling the flood until
it bursts free meandering
to reclaim its older path.

From there, earth is cut away
by water snaking around
dipping under fallen trunks
sidling past the heaps of brush
that washed down from neighborhoods
on the other side of town.

Floating toys will take the ride
before fast grip can gather
escaping backyards during
the sudden-rising storm surge.

Here in the wooded silence,
beyond the noisy traffic,
they pile up in the tangles
waiting rescue that won't come.
The squirrels take no notice,
and muskrat finds no delight.

Here in the purgatory
of lost objects they pass time
until other hands find them,
or greater floods send them on.

Xanthophyll, Anthocyanin, and Carotene

Xanthophyll, anthocyanin, and carotene
how clinical the pigments sound
shunning mystery for accuracy.

How stunning in autumn sunlight
as the greens surrender
and the trees put on
yellow, red, and orange,
colors a child could name.

My Last Walk

My last walk takes me along the highway,
a path so straight no four-legged creature would forge.
Nothing more than a train bed stripped of rail and tie,
trying to go wild.

Traffic floods my ears,
but not my eyes.
Walls of tree and shrub
rise towering left and right
like Charlton Heston at the Red Sea,
not Moses at the *yam suph*,
an adventure without special effects.

This path is becoming real
with howling wind and shaking bows.
Birds gone to cover flushed at my approach,
but this is their place now.
I, the invader, who had not come to conquer.

A trail of lasts:
last blue chicory staring up from swirling leaves,
last of the sumacs' red foliage with cone-shaped parapets guarding the flank,
monarchs too weak for Mexico looking for the last of the milkweed.
And the berries of white and blue and red,
Dogwood, grapes, haw, and a fruit
so red-ripe a grownup would warn against tasting.
Boys deserve such warnings,
fears grow slower than feet.
These last grapes were small
too bitter, I thought, but still, I tasted
sour and mostly seed from a summer beyond dry.
A boy would eat them,
one who had sworn a childhood oath to run away.
Never would the clan be broken without an escape to the wood
eating berries and fruits like woodland tribes.

These last fruits belong to others now,
to birds lying hunkered in the bushes,
the worst eaten last,
fruit for desperation of a spring delayed.

Groundhog

There was a groundhog on the trail,
dead,
without any visible marks,
still.
The road runs so close
he could have been bluntly struck
only to race this far,
not knowing the death he carried
in his body.
Knowing, he might have preferred
to die here in a place of solitude
without fume
waiting for me to walk by.

Maybe my imagination plays tricks
and he came gently to this
spot to sleep,
stepping out of his body
as a friend of death
recognizing what
he and I have always carried in our bodies
and taking the lighter path.

It's Colder this Morning

It's colder this morning as I walk toward the river.
Not so cold, yet, that the trees have shaken color.
That comes later and I will wade knee-deep
through the discarded fabric of their splendor.

It isn't wind that robs them; they surrender freely.
Through summer gale I have seen them grip petiole
against the onslaught, but once the day sends the chill
they push them off to flutter down in silence.
Even a still day sees them quietly relinquish
what they held so severely against the blast.

It is the cold that drives this barren cause.
Then they turn to cheat the freeze with branches so bare
that winter's fury can't grasp. Stripped of all but self,
they cast slim shadows of wind and light.
Foliage will bloom again in spring fashion,
but twig and branch are life and not dropped easily.
They do not think or feel, I am told,
but pruned, they burst from new bud,
as if nurtured by wound and pain,
purpose without intention, life from earth.

Along the Shore

The trees along the shore
took off their green
and the sky threaded
a blue ribbon between the trunks.

Fall, a season of paths
where spaces open through
the underbrush and the
wooded wall becomes a way.

Winter Is So Much Softer

Winter is so much softer
when I see it from my window.
The furnace comes on with a cool draft
in advance of heated air.
It's not the chill of real wind
that sets the teeth rattling
and skin to rise,
every hair alert.
Real winter is just beyond the pane
and I watch, hardly touched by it.
Even with hand on glass I sense the cold
but do not enter it,
or hardly enter.
Such a warm game to watch the winter,
pretending to be there
in shirt sleeves
observing swirling snow,
but not knowing any of it.

Wakefield

There were
tracks in the new snow
(a squirrel most likely
by the way he'd
hopped from
one drift
to another).
I mused over following
the imprints to
where they ended
perhaps with a frozen corpse
or warm leaf-den
stranded on bare limbs.
I gave up the thought
figuring I'd lose him
in the spring or
under newer snow.

Not Like Jesus

River is frozen,
in sunlight the gulls alight,
ice shines like white sand.

Cat creeps across frozen flood
walks on water–not Jesus.

Sky

Last Time I Spoke with the Moon

The last time I spoke with the moon,
   it gave me no answer.
"What makes you so smug?" I said.
Nothing came but the silvery wash of silence.
It was fully awake, but even a canine's howl
   could not entice speech from it.

What taunt could touch this lesser light?
"The sun would answer," I chided.
   (But I knew that I would never willingly look into that face.)
The moon knew too as it lulled along its silent path.

"You listen, but you do not speak!"

Nothing.

"If you spoke, I would listen!"

Nothing.

"If we both spoke, neither could listen!"

Nothing.

"If we both listened, neither would speak!"

"I hear it too."

The silvery wash of silence.

Under Sail

The water talks to me
in measured rhythms
of wave against hull.
Its beat stirs a gull
from her fascination
with a floating meal.
She has been wary of my approach,
wondering how close I will come,
or if my desire is for her prize.
The white sails are my wings,
but I am bound to the intersection
of wind and wave;
I can go no higher.
Gull knows my earthbound frame.
Grudgingly she unfolds her arms
mounting up, embracing sky.
She takes to air, circles the mast,
and sets down in her place.
She cries out to tell me
I am only an annoyance.
Her voice syncopates the
rhythm of the water.

My Sky

When I look up,
the sky is mine.
It is no bigger than I
because it can
be caressed and held close
like a lover,
and still bigger
so that freedom is
soaring in hot currents
where there are no
directions, no course plotting,
no up or down or
earth to abort life.
Just sky,
to be touched
and molded until
its breath is mine
and my lungs hold in
blue air
then let it go
to run after with
new life.

Morning

It is morning,
and the deck is wet with dew.
The air is crisp
and my life opens in the silence.
A Great Blue wades along the near shore.
At first,
I think he is watching me,
then, not.
His neck swiftly uncoils
and he's snared
a shiny fish.
He takes a new stance.
So still, he stands between
energy and matter,
between flashes of lightning reaction
and the serene pause.
Then it is finished.
He opens his wings and lifts to the sky
more pteranodon than avian.
He tips on the wind and I nod back.
It is morning,
and the deck is wet with dew.
My life opens in silence.

Flight

From my cell, I see the clouds,
but feel no wind,
no breath to wash me clean.
Falcon is not envious of fume or power,
but I of her,
For she wings free, soaring with silent strokes
in an ocean of air.

What does she see?
Is it hare or mouse or shadow of light?
Can she see beyond the light,
and glimpse her own circle of self?

Falcon is no dreamer, she just wings free,
and in that, is more wise than I,
with fewer fears and no remorse.

But does she love?
And if love bears the price of other emotions,
I will love,
I will fly free,
I will soar as Falcon in an ocean of air.

The Turning

The geese are calling
early this year, and
urging
sluggish wings to flight after a
season of gleaning fatness from the fields.
They protest as they mount upward,
then fall into rhythm
with one voice
calling a cadence
for beating wings.
Their complaints
fall away
in precise formation.
The season changes.

Cat on the Ice

A cat walks
on the frozen river
her big belly
swollen with kittens.
They cry out hungrily within
as she watches gulls
standing à la mode.
I call to her;
she hunkers down.
Distrust is the edge of survival.
Lives on instinct
and birds
slow to flight.

17 December 1903

Along an open stretch of sandy shore
two brothers breathed the dream of human flight.
With canvas-covered frame they stood before
the wind which lifted time and forward sight
in views unseen by an earth-bound race.
What fears were theirs who gravity defied
whether stretched on wing or standing in place?
The toss of a coin determined the ride,
but both held forth that day to trust unknown.
They saw the work of hand and mind revealed
when engine sang and wings lifted over foam
in birdless flight with human fears concealed.
Earth flew on frail wing that December day
when sky became a place for human play.

Red Huffy

Pedaling with fury
of wheeling sprocket
racing downhill
adding muscle
to accelerating
free fall,
then standing
full height
levitating on pedals
above the earth,
hot air rising from
freshly rolled asphalt
becoming hot wind
rushing over
arms outstretched
in balance
without grip.
I am become
the cyclist
who invented flight.
My brother
only watches with envy
as my red Huffy
blurs in a jetting
streak of imagination.

Time

Black Hole

So dense even light cannot escape
sucking everything into its gravity
pulling all variety of matter
into one dot of space.
Time compresses into a thing,
one thing
with everything else,
real,
solid,
one.
Until, with word of power
all light is scattered,
one becomes many,
energy becomes matter,
time begins.

Watching

Bill had a watch
and an airplane made out of a white bull's horn.
The watch in his pocket,
the plane in a corner cupboard
behind glass shutters
where a boy could not reach.

Bill was a mystery,
my Gammy's husband with my last name,
but not a grandfather.
Gammy said his real name was Polish,
but took the name "Smith."
More American, he thought.

My Grandpa Smith
came from Glasgow
and called the name "Scottish."
He was always a stranger,
probably a watch in his pocket, too
but buried before my father was nine.

Bill's watch was not gone.
It came out like
a magic talisman,
always a delight
at the end of a chain.
Beneath the shiny cover,
a white face with crisp black features,
X, V, and I's.

For years I wore a watch on a wrist
shackled to time.
Now, like a smooth stone,
time lives in my pocket.
I open it
and look into its eye,
not to see it,
but to be connected,
to Bill, to Gammy,
to a bull's horn that looked like
it might fly.

Night Train

Darkness meets darkness
at the glass wall that divides
the still black of the sleeping travelers
from the glittering smooth,
ebony world that slides
past with clatter of wheels.

The night wanders free
consuming light and life,
while two steel bars stretch
to pull me their captive.

I open the window.

A different blackness meets
stale air,
and the smell of the land
becomes my breath.
The night is a part of me.

I sleep, then wake.

In the distance
a single lighted window,
and for a moment
I shared that light,
and the rails,
and then the darkness.

Remembering Clocks

I am old enough to remember clocks
that ticked at night,
lying in bed,
sleepless.
Their beat was the interminable
drumming of a distant
enemy mocking my consciousness,
or the sometimes steady
drip, drip, drip
of a Chinese water torture
that drives mad and ends all hope of dreaming.
There is no ticking tonight,
just the faint green glow of the digital face.
My eyes,
so adjusted to the dark,
see shadows cast on the wall
by its glimmer.
Ticking was, at least a voice,
a companion in its time,
reminding me of the moments sliding helplessly away.
Tonight time flows silently
sleuthing away hours,
slowly without a cadence
that counts the tasks left undone.
By day, it flies.
Yet, from day to day, so little seems to change
and I am back under the green glow.
Sometimes I think that time doesn't change anything
until I see myself in the mirror.
I will not fight this time.
Like the child's game,
it will come,
ready or not.

Time

Keep it.
Mark it.
Save it.
Do as you like,
but the words do not fit
and prove false.
It will not hold the stain
when marked,
never kept on a string,
or pocketed with change.
Not ours forever.
Keeps us.
Marks us,
passes us into the ages.

I Remember Her Much Taller

I remember her much taller
than she was.
Of course I was only six
and everyone was tall,except my little brother.
In the pantry was a calendar with a beautiful princess,
crowned with tiara, face framed with rosy cheeks,
but not a princess, Elizabeth,
her royal highness.
My grandmother was Elisabeth, too,
her only claim on royalty,
a sister,
a cook's assistant at Balmoral.
At Grandma's house
another form of
nurture reigned.
To lost boys came
biscuits from brightly colored tins,
white tea,
and buttery shortbreads.

The kitchen was bright and sunny
on the second floor.
Out in the hall,
was a picture of a Sunday school class.
My class.
I remember the day it was taken,
and why I sat
so angelically
next to the teacher
while the others
played to the camera
or ran amuck.
Donnie, Billy, Glen, and Wendy,
the names of childhood friends
nearly gone from memory.

My mother dressed me for that picture,
not without protest,
wearing white shirt, bowtie,
　　open jacket, short pants,
　　　　and Buster Browns.

I hated wearing shorts.
Men did not wear them,
why should I at four?
I didn't want my picture taken,
knees bared in so unmanly a way.
I sat by the teacher,
out of center.
"Out," the teacher said, "of the camera's eye."
She had lied in church that day,
the day I sat on the outside of my own world
and watched children being children
while I sat as a man,
bare kneed and alone.
I don't know if my mother ever saw the photo.
In time, it came to define me in my Grandma world,
but so did the biscuits and tea
and the wey
she sang tae us,
"Lizbeth.

Fear

As a child
I did not appreciate fear.
Oh, there were
baby fears
of dark basements
haunted by hulking
furnaces with
long arms of gravity-fed
cold air returns.
They were just pipes
and shadows.
They did not hit like the Toughs
who thought me a small, safe target.
Only twice did
any land the stinging blow.
I remember their reactions,
both the same,
though years apart.
I must not have done it right,
not to suit them.
After straight shot to face,
they stopped,
heads turning to silent companions,
as if their attempt at improvisation
had left the story-line.
I failed the audition.
Was I to fall?
or cry?
or run?

Like an idiot,
I did nothing.
They should have told me.
I just stood my ground
and they wondered if I had
seen the stars.
I had,
but not enough to appreciate fear.
No second punch ever found me,
and the two traced
wide circles around me after that
as if I knew the secret of
their souls,
the boy who didn't
fall,
or fight,
or run.
In time, fear found me.
I see the ones I love
at a distance
where fate makes helpless.
Easier to take the blow
and stand-down
the bully.

Pittsburgh

How different today,
parking on Mount Washington,
taking the Incline down into the valley.
The old train station is now a boutique mall;
the waitress at lunch laughed easily.

Coming back,
the sky framed a perfect postcard
with colors sliding back into the rivers
to define the Point.

No smoke in the valley.
Not like the days when my grandfather
rode this track into smoldering
steam from the mills,
fume of open hearth,
the descent into hell.

The laborers came back up,
armed with black lunch pails already emptied
into hungry stomachs,
faces darkened with sweat-molded soot.

It was work, not penance
that took them down to the coke fires,
and obstinate pride that lifted them back
at shift's end.

No Time for Angst

My first car was a Rambler,
flathead six,
mostly rust
when I took its wheel.
But the front seat flipped
down into a bed,
not that I needed it
for submarine races,
still,
there in case.
Angst was not making it
with grades,
with girls,
and Nam was in the headlines
and the back of nineteen-year-old minds.
It was not assumed
that things would break right
if the cash was good,
or mommy and daddy made it so.
Rights were opposites of lefts,
and choice was to please the Dean
or go to Uncle.
Do or die.
Many did both.
No time for angst,
just choices.

Barber Shopping

Karl's Barber Shop was a man's place
with an inviolate code of conduct.
Each knew his place in the rotation.
"First in, first up" was the only rule,
and "Next" was the call to the plate.
Karl and Joe umpired the procession,
and boys could play, their bikes leaning
against the brick wall in the alley.
The barber pole twisted red, white, and blue,
and rotating chrome chairs dangled straps
for honing straight razor's edge with
rhythmic slap of steel on leather.
Fearless Fosdick stared down from
comic posters, hat tipped, hair slicked,
and bullet holes with hovering flies.

My wife and I now go together,
there's a list to sign as we walk in.
The room smells of scratch and sniff roses
that live in a pile of magazines.
No greaseless Wildroot,
but an apricot/peach something.
Cassie doesn't look like a barber,
prettier than Karl without talk of
fish, football, or the eighth inning.
The time here is not the same,
not better or worse, just different,
a different thing altogether.

The Bonapartes Landed

The Bonapartes landed
shaking off their black crowns
for winter plumage.
The Ring-bills wonder how long they will stay,
So do I
as the world becomes sleepy.
It will be a fitful sleep
with the children off to war.
The gulls are not sleeping.
They make a mess of the empty docks
and sit in their army array,
Ring-billed and Bonaparte
waiting for a Waterloo
or another migration.
Yesterday, I saw a Coot swimming
near the edge of the basin
passing itself off as a duck,
minding its own business.
Too bad about the name.
Holy in its way.

Last Dance

I saw a man stop dancing.
It was at the bar and a band was playing,
a good band.
The regulars came to dance
and drink,
and laugh,
and make up stories
that got bigger
with the amplified beat of the bass guitar.
An older man was there,
not much older.

He had come to dance

All in black,
two-tone shoes,
silver buckle
he had the moves.
He and his partner did not miss a step
until
he just stopped.
Would have gone down hard
but for the woman in his arms
who gently floated at his side.
Dance floor suddenly clear
and the squad repeating
"Clear."
Three times they shocked him
before sliding him onto a body board,
gurneying him out the door

He had come to dance.

Patterns

Memento, homo, quia pulvis es et in pulverem reverteris

Memento,
Remember the days of dust
when no smell was sweeter
than wet, black earth.
When babes
stepped forward out of the
dust of sand castles,
and the sun baked
the fortress
white and sugary.

Reverteris,
that's the trick.
Remembering counts too little.
It's the going back
that's tough.

Memento– Revererteris.
Reverteris– Memento.
Walk the castles carefully.
Sugar is weak mortar
and the bucket-molded towers
don't remember;
they just revert.
We walk the ledges
'til the sweetness
between our toes
becomes the weak enemy,
and there's nothing
to separate feet from enemy.
The seam disappears.
Man– Dust
Dust– Man

I am the wet ground.
The dust will remember.

Memento, pulvis, quia homo.

Mandala

Today I was caught up
in a moment when it seemed
that I could touch the earth
and feel that it was
ready to be touched and
formed and moved
until it took a shape that
was not its own,
but an idea
that could count all things
as one,
and yet be everything.
Nowhere was this any more visible
than on the horizon.
Whether I stood back or close,
all was near,
flowing in a
singular separateness
that divided nothing,
not even time,
but made eternal moments
held by the
vastness of space
and the finitude of mind.

With new awareness I felt this,
and when eternity ended,
the moments slid
apart and I was left
in a shadow
while life called with
voices heard in dreams.

New Tomorrow

Catbird, what will be new tomorrow?
Will brown sky meet us?
Will we call it new,
or call it sky?
No new sky.
"Tomorrow is today a day later,"
so calls the bird
with yesterday's song
and voice sweet enough
to make earth weep.
Wind speaks to tree,
tree to earth,
earth finds comfort,
but the word is not new.
Earth hears it well
and sends shoots to
pierce sky with wing and flight.
No new sky.
One child new,
only one.
Enough
Bird, sky, tree, earth, shoots, wing, child.
I will be new.
All are new.

I Didn't Know You

I didn't know you
except after death,
and for this I'm glad
because now life won't
prove me wrong
when I try to remember
what you ought to have been.

Let's let that be for now,
you, the product of my creation
and me, the product of yours.
Apart from us, we really don't exist,
unless someone else has remembering,
but from what I've seen,
the world forgets,
and then I'm no better
for opening my eyes and making
your life go.
Then I'm all that's left
and there's not enough to
fill the living for two that
must be in one.

Strange how life and death
follow patterns that can't
be followed by the eye,
but only by the forgetting
and the remembering.
And if forgotten,
we're dead.
Unless someone else can recall
the numbers of hair
and the living we kept in our minds.

The Elements of the Universe

The elements of the universe
know nothing
of their being,
and yet, they speak of being.
They exist as a word that is spoken,
a word so real that
all other voices
seem muted.
My silence in all this seems
unnatural. For being endowed
with heart
and mind, lips and tongue,
I speak less eloquently,
with less faith and vigor,
but perhaps not with less hope.
For it is within hope I find
true humanity, and join
in the silent speech
of the created order.

Persephone Rides on Laughter

Persephone rides on laughter.
Her beauty brings the spring,
her playfulness carries the
scent of new grass.

Had I wondered where laughter went,
I should have known when I
went searching for the friend of my youth.
For in you it breathes so easily,
like the spring,
like the scent of new grass.

Wander with me
fair and free
through meadows,
and along fresh paths,
until the laughter greets us
and our hearts are one.

More Tests

They want more tests
to test the results of the last test
that might not be right.
The tests never make well.
They sow fright to make themselves important
and everything hinges on them.
Joy is getting word that nothing was found.
Six months, test again,
maybe three (just to be safe!)
Of course, nothing is our latest hope.
Life is managing the spaces between
the nothing and the may be
something.

Fear is the driver,
fear of death.
Who named him that,
the one who has always walked beside?
Do they think tests can chase him off
or have they been merely counting laps to the finish,
waiting for a checkered flag?
Death is the faithful companion,
the one never-forsaking friend,
always has been.
I carry him in me.
He is my teacher who tells me to live until
        there is only one
                next reasonable step
                        over the invisible threshold.

Some take another roll,
hedging bets with a test.

Machines feed well on fearful flesh.

Without Purpose

I am going to learn to walk without purpose,
to stop halfway down the sidewalk
and talk to myself
with animated gestures.
I will always linger long enough
so that everyone who views
the surveillance camera
knows that I have no cell phone.
Someday they will all know me
In the malls,
parking lots,
and public buildings.
"Poor bastard," they will call me,
"Harmless," too.
They will ask each other
if I have gone off my medication,
or if I have ever been truly diagnosed.
Seeing me thus,
they will cease to see me at all.
I suppose watching neighbors
is always easier than knowing.
In the end, the spectators
are deluded.

Eucharist

Life comes,
with no holding on.
We see and feel
until the aching for it
lifts it from the table.
There is no drinking,
only seeing.
"I thirst," cries a voice,
but lips are weak arms.
The cup is too high,
too shiny,
and the polish burns against
raw flesh.
The only drink is tears and sweat,
the only cup the sunken eyes
and cheeks.

The drink is in the thirsting.
Life is not held,
only let go.

Covenant with the Dead

To Edith

Death came long, but suddenly,
and now it doesn't matter
because our secret is kept
and there'll be no more telling.

But then I told you
it would be that way,
and you seemed pleased
that one so young
would know a tale of the old.

So now you're past dying,
but I am left
the bearer of half a secret.
Your half's still good
though I heard a whisper of it
when you left.

No bother though,
it's still safe,
or will be
when I come across.

Mazes

Wandering in mazes of our own making,
we stumble in places we did not choose.

The twists of the labyrinth
set us swimming in confusion,
one path turns into two,
then disappears into a solid wall.

Was there not a time
when this was a child's game?
A riddle to be solved,
a problem clothed in boxwood hedges
for an afternoon's delight?

In that garden was laughter,
and a key to the puzzle.
What was it?
Keep a hand against the wall,
and the path will not turn
back on itself.
Was that it?

But the walls of this maze play tricks,
and a hand would not rest well against it.
A hand to hold would serve better.
Here's mine.

The Night Seemed Longer

The night seemed longer than usual
and still no word
had come to them.
So they waited for
sign or sound,
but the streets were silent
and empty.
The children were in bed, but not
dreaming of sugarplums,
just dreaming.
The air was still
and hot and mixed with the smell of the
closeness of life,
and the emptiness of the streets echoed the silence.

A new baby cried
for the first time.
The night air
still hung heavy over the town,
but now the emptiness of the streets
echoed the cry.

Hope Comes in a Wooden Box

Hope comes in a wooden box,
and it came
crying because there was
no one to pay
for being born,
so dying,
or living became the
payment.

Other than that
there was nothing
except the
scared
bunch
that left him standing
on a hill
with nothing to do
but take whatever came,
wine or spit.

I can't remember more.
He came in a wooden box
and we tried
to send him out the same way.
Some say there was a
mix-up
and he didn't leave at all.

Love

Town Gossip

I met our neighbor today
at the convenience store.
I was for coffee,
she, for scratching a lottery card.
Anyway, she asked if we were rich
just blurted it out,
like she always does
straight-out.

I must have smiled,
mostly at the predictable bluntness.
Next week she'll ask again
not remembering the old path,
but she took the smile as a "Yes,"
so I had to question,
"What does it mean to be rich?"

Turning nosiness into philosophy is an art
I don't possess,
but what does it mean?
We don't owe much.
We eat so that we mind the scales
and walk off calories.
I know enough rich people.
In big houses they talk poor
as they try to gather more.
Still, it feels as though we have enough
just with each other.
So if you hear the rumor that we're rich,
it's gossip.
Probably true.

Darfur

Being born human,
compassion should come easy
as my kin sit in the waste of war,
sisters and brothers of one flesh.

Compassion should come easy,
but I live in isolation of
sisters and brothers of one flesh,
voices calling in need.

But I live in isolation of
soft music that covers their cry,
voices calling in need
I, who have ears to hear.

Soft music covers their cry
as my kin sit in the waste of war,
I, who have ears to hear,
being born human.

No Forgiveness

There's an electric motor in my toothbrush.
It drones at me when it needs to be recharged,
and I obey more than the hygienist's plea
for me to floss regularly. She knows well
that I do not, but she will still always ask.
I rinse and spit myself clean for six more months.
The motor shakes my jaw like a jackhammer
and offers no forgiveness if I talk back.

Alzheimer

He looked at her voice,
for there he hoped to recognize her.
Dim eyes betray awareness,
but the voice was still real.
Names no longer matter,
gone with all faces.

He looked at her voice.

Familiar, comforting, without face or name.

He looked at her voice,
but not as one tracing the wispy breath of a cold morning,
those were images of sight,
they belonged to the eyes.

When memory and vision fade,
one only sees with the ears and remembers with the heart.

He looked at her voice.

What was it? It was familiar, it was safe.

"Don't worry, I'm here!"

Escape to Poetry

The story nags at me as I sit at my desk.
The characters cry that they
long for life, for action,
and they tire of waiting for me.
I tell them to go ahead without me,
but they never do.
When I do sit with them, they won't listen.
They push me along when I want to linger
on a sunset or feel the burning run
of a line racing through bare hands.
"Hurry," they urge as if my fingers
could fly fast enough
to add pulse to their
already racing hearts.
What do they want from me besides life?
"It's a small thing," they argue,
but it sounds like nagging to me.
They never do what I want
and the chapter leaves
them hanging less than me.
I swear that I love them,
but sometimes I betray,
secretly stealing myself away.
I make the excuses of a faithless partner,
"It's their fault, they demand so much,
day after day, they drive me to another," I say.
She will be kind and soft.
She makes no demands,
holds me in her arms,
and tells me how abused I am.
I want to receive her words,
and, even more, the way of her touch.
"Just a few short lines," she whispers,
not even asking me to speak her name.
We meet only in the discretion
of a quiet time together
when the world of senses
overwhelms self
and we are alone,
without the voices,
without the nagging,
without the story.
Just poetry.

Milkweed

A child running,
arms flailing
to catch the drifting seed,
the Santa Claus seed
as light as a feather,
as white as the snow.

In cupped hands
the treasure rests,
framed by soft fingers
darkened by the sootiness
of boy play.

Now he whispers the wish
beyond his power to secure,
the magical words now risked to
be spoken aloud.

Then upward he flings his hands,
the swirling puff circles,
drifts,
and catches currents.
Without sound,
beyond sight,
it is gone.

Whatever became of the hopes of a boy?

Have they become
the food of caterpillars,
the shelter of a chrysalis,
the stalk for the unfolding
of wet sticky wings?
Or is the whisper of magic
that takes its own wings,
and drifts and floats until
it finds another hand to hold it?
Another heart to listen?

Beyond Horizons

Beyond horizons,
      the sun rises and sets.
Beyond horizons,
      the eyes wander until
the unseen takes shape,
      and the world is formed.

To speak of things unseen is to dream.
Dreams are the mother of hope,
      and her children are my sisters.
Dreams birth the colors of a new dawn,
      and the dawn is my brother.

Why should I fear my brother,
      or my sister?
Am I not also a child of dreams?

I stand at the dawn.
My heart holds hope.
My life speaks the dream.

Quiet Time

The flesh of your thigh
feels warm beneath my touch.
My senses are awash with
the fragrance of our bodies'
communion.
After the passion,
it is still you I love.

Truth Aloud

Words without feelings
are sounds to be heard and
nothing more.
If woven in syllables alone,
the artist may be seen.
If crafted in beauty,
the skill is discerned,
but without feeling the heart
remains unknown.
A lie spoken beautifully remains untrue.
A truth unspoken may starve a hungry soul.
So I offer the truth,
plainly spoken,
without craft or skill:
I am a man.
I love you.

She Asked Me What I Thought

She asked me what I thought,
but long ago,
I knew that I would like her.
Should I tell her,
tell her that her eyes
say more about her heart
than she might want this stranger to know?

She asked me what I thought
about the clutter of a room,
but I see only ties to friends
at a distance,
that she holds on to love,
and her eyes say more
than she might want this stranger to know.

I wonder what she thinks,
when I call for no reason
except to hear her voice?
Long ago,
I knew that I would like her,
but does she see, in my eyes, more
than I might want this stranger to know?

If I Scare You

If I scare you,
come closer,
and let me hold you.
There are many paths
that we could walk,
many ways to travel.
To chose one or the other
matters less
than walking together.
Dreams are better
hand in hand,
your hand
and my hand.
Do I scare you?
Come closer,
love casts out fear

If We Were Children

If we were children, would the world even wonder
As we walked together?
Would anyone notice our laughter, except for a
smiling sky and shapeless clouds
amused as we pointed at each wisp and spoke a name?

There is still a child in me.

If we were children, would the world even wonder
As minutes ticked into hours,
and the silence between words sang for joy?
Would either of us mourn the missed suppers?
The street lights awakened as daylight slips into night?
The shroud of darkness, and the stars that smile?

There is still a child in me.

If we were children, would the world even wonder
if I took your hand for a moment?
There is so much to see that is new,
so much to see that is fresh and undiscovered and true.
Or are you the one who is fresh, and undiscovered, and true?

Don't laugh that I see you like this,
Children see everything differently.

There is still a child in me.

Reflections

A Long-time Affair

It's often said that Americans are in love with the automobile. In this regard, I am, evidently, not very patriotic. My affair has been with the bicycle.

If you asked me to list all the cars that I've driven over the years, I'd have to give it quite a bit of thought. As far as bikes go, there have been only three, all red, all perfect.

My first bike was a twenty-inch Huffy Convertible. I learned to ride a "big boy's" bike on that Huffy. I had tried the training wheel route, but those proved pretty useless. Not only did they set the bicycle at an odd angle, they reduced the cornering ability to that of a double-brick semi.

My Huffy was the bike that my father ran behind while I kept saying, "don't let go!"

Of course, he did. (You never really ride until the runner lets go.) Actually, you've never really ridden until you are wheeling downhill, pedaling full speed on a twenty-inch Huffy. I think it was no accident that the Wright Brothers were bicycle builders. Years later, when I lived in Dayton, Ohio, I learned more about the famous brothers and about the Huffmans whose Davis Sewing Machine Company became Huffy. The Huffmans also owned a field out east of Dayton, and it was on Huffman Prairie that the brothers actually perfected their Flyer. The entire history of flight was reenacted as I rode down Cain Street in Youngstown, Ohio, waving to my earthbound younger brother. With hands free and arms extended, I had surely invented flight.

My brother's revenge would come when I was eight years old and he abandoned his three-wheeler. The prospects were not good. My older sister had received a second hand-me-down bike from a cousin. She couldn't ride two, and my brother was a six year old novice. The math was simple. I was to inherit a blue twenty-six inch *girl's* bike. I was told that I had "outgrown" the beautiful, sporty, red, speedy, classic-lined Huffy Convertible.

"You're getting too big for this little bike" is a lie most boys would want to hear, but I didn't believe a word of it! I knew what "too big" looks like on a twenty inch bike. It was a gangly teenager whose knees threaten to rearrange a jawbone with each half cycle of the sprocket wheel. That was not me. As an adult, I am a towering five foot seven; as a child, however, I was on the short side. My sister and I would walk down Indianola to catch the Market Street bus downtown on Saturday mornings. I was eight, she was twelve, and the bus driver thought I was under six and wouldn't accept my nickel fare. I even stood tall and said that I was eight, but he didn't flinch. Wounded pride is worth more than five cents. Even worse about being short in elementary school was the narrow field of girls about the same size, but that's another story.

I knew my only cycling option was to swallow the last of my pride and ride the bar-less blue bike with the wire basket in front of the handlebars. My father said he'd remove the basket and bolt a bar across the chasm between the yoke and the seat. The bike would still be blue, like me, and my imagination did not do me any favors in that regard. I could hear the jeers about riding my *sister's* bike. I couldn't even threaten them with a big brother who would beat them up. My sister probably could, but that would have defeated the purpose.

As providence would have it, the family received free passes to Myers Lake Amusement Park. It was the day the park was opened to telephone employees. With admission came raffle tickets and intermittent sequences of numbers read over the loud speakers. That was the day my number was up! The prize was a new, red, shiny, twenty-six inch Murray *boy's* bike. My sister said that I really didn't win the bike, but my father did and gave it to me because I needed one. I, however, knew the truth. God wanted me to have that bike.

Don't get me wrong, I loved my twenty-inch Huffy Convertible. It was small, compact, and quick. The Murray had balloon tires and weighed as much as I did. It was the Humvee of bikes in the 1950s. It was awesome. My problem was logistics. Even with the seat at the lowest position, I could not remain seated and keep my feet on the pedals at the lowest point of rotation. The solution was simple; I rode standing up. Later in life I had two children, so the strategy had no lasting effect.

The other two problems called for more innovation. Being too short to pedal the bike meant that I was too short to throw my leg over the bar and ride off. To get on the Murray, I had to begin at the front step or curb or any place that I could take a step up. Sometimes I had to walk the Behemoth quite a distance before starting, and then I had to work hard to catch up to the others who could take off on the spot. My final strategy was derived from TV westerns. Like Hopalong Cassidy, I learned to place my left foot in the stirrup and swing into the saddle. In this case, it meant rotating the sprocket until I could place my left foot on the pedal. With two pushes from the right leg, I usually had enough forward momentum to mount the beast, usually. When I fell, it was only practice for the second major problem, the dismount.

For the quick dismount, gravity is a friend. For the painless dismount, gravity is the enemy. When the bike is shiny and new, the added difficulty is to find the correct balance between a controlled crash and minimum property damage. A perfect landing was to maneuver back to the front step and brake fast enough to catch the step under the left foot. Failing that, the landscaping was my bike's friend. I would aim my bike toward a bush or hedge and bail out at the last minute. In this way, the Murray rarely hit the ground. My sister and her friends were a bit of an annoyance. As I approached, they would stop whatever they were doing to catch the next act. To this day, she reminds me of my application of small boys with big bikes.

After the fourth grade, our family moved to North Olmsted on the west side of Cleveland. The streets were flatter than in Youngstown and my legs had grown considerably longer. As a result, the plantings around the new house thrived.

The guys in the new neighborhood had lighter bikes. The red Murray with its balloon tires still outweighed the medium-weight Schwinns that Rich and Ronnie used. Still, I could run over any curb with no ill effects (though with my history of riding, recklessness was not a consideration). Greg had the fastest bike, an English Racer. With three gears and skinny tires its middle name was *speed*. With handbrakes instead of coaster brakes, it could be pedaled backwards with no effect except a clicking ratchet sound that told all the panting racers that the finish line had already been crossed.

Still, the red Murray was a reliable trip maker. Since my father will probably not be reading this account, I will confess to at least one trek across Westlake and Bay Village to the shores of Lake Erie. As I approached sixteen, my appreciation of my bike wavered for a brief time.

For a year or so, my brother and I got up at 5:30 a.m. to deliver the morning paper, the Plain Dealer. Except for snow days, our bikes carried us. There were two inescapable truths to consider, however. First, there was not much profit in the newspaper business (at least not in our end of the trade) and second, an eight-year-old balloon-tired bike was not a *chick magnet*. Cars were, and I found a 1952 Ford Coupe for sale at the gas station for fifty dollars. I had that much money, along with all the amassed logic of a sixteen year old brain. I explained to my father how it would all work for the benefit of humanity and probably bring an end to the Cold War. He calmly explained gasoline, insurance, and how a car will "nickel and dime you." No *chick magnet* for me. When I started dating, it would have to be with a brown Buick station wagon set to midnight curfew time.

By now I had a real job as an orderly in the research lab at Fairview General Hospital. It was a great gig for a high school kid, and I probably put in as many hours volunteering as I did on payroll. Still, work was five miles from home and my father drove the wagon to work. On school days, I could take the city bus and be picked up by my Dad on the way home at night. Weekends and vacations meant that I would need my own set of wheels, two of them.

My next love appeared to me in a vision. Actually, it was a picture in a Western Auto Catalogue. The Sherwood Flyer was not a deluxe bike. It did not have white walls, but it had all the essentials. It was everything my sturdy Murray was not. It had skinny tires, handbrakes, and three gears that changed with a twist of the right-hand grip. It was even imported from England by Western Flyer, so it was an *English Racer*. It cost me thirty-nine ninety-five plus tax in 1964. As an accessory, I bought a generator light. With a click of a latch, the rear tire would turn a small generator which produced enough current to light a headlamp and a taillight. That's what I used to travel Lorain Road through city traffic after dark. The old Murray was given a good home. A surgical technician at the hospital rebuilt it and took to riding during lunch breaks.

The red Sherwood Flyer has been with me ever since. It has survived child carriers bolted to its frame and a daughter who used to ride it to gymnastics at the YMCA. By then, it was twenty-eight years old, and from what my daughter tells me, the boys at the "Y" had never seen anything quite like it. From her perspective, the thing worked quite well as a *guy magnet*. Go figure!

In 2007, my Sherwood is approaching forty-three years old. It looks pretty much the same having avoided the short-legged fate of my Murray. The red finish has faded some from sunlight. In places, the patina has turned "desert bronze" (the color of our '63 Buick wagon). I only live four blocks from Lake Erie and the ride there will not get me into any trouble. On the other hand, when the road is flat and empty ahead of me, I can still let go of the handle grips and coast that red bike as if reinventing flight.

Funeral Arrangements

My older sister, younger brother, and I were part of the funeral arrangements when our mother died. Being nearly four, I wasn't in on the actual discussions and, in all fairness, they were trying to protect us by keeping life normal. My sister was sent to school the day my mother died, but only made it through half the day. She was eight and later attended the services. My two-year-old brother and I were spared the emotional trauma.

Sometime in the arrangement process, the decision was made to farm-out the children. My brother and I went to stay with one aunt and uncle; they were older than my parents and had a childless marriage. My sister went with another of Dad's brothers and his wife. They already had a daughter, and my older sister could learn a new role as younger sister.

I do not remember much from those days. It seemed like we were fussed over too much. I remember missing my sister, being curious about my mill-worker uncle's rough Lava hand soap, and wondering when my father would pick us up from this vacation. Once we visited my sister who seemed to be having fun living with our cousin. When I was in my forties, an aunt told me that I used to go to every woman in our family gatherings, look them in the eye, and ask, "Are you my mother?"

I never did find her. My father broke ranks when he realized that in addition to losing a wife, he had now lost his children. While Uncle Ollie and Aunt Helen were, from then on, my second parents, it was good to go home. My sister took on the role of mother hen; my father cooked, cleaned and supervised a string of housekeepers whose job it was to be home with us after school. My sister was in public school. This was before daycare centers, and my brother and I went to the Salvation Army day school while my dad was at work. I remember that quite well. We churned butter once, and I had to sit in the corner because I was not good at naps in the middle of the day.

There was little doubt that my sister was in charge. My dad could hire the housekeepers, but we could run off the mean ones in a matter of days. In management terms, we had an "informal" management structure. In other words, the people at the top thought they were making the decisions, but the real arrangements were made on the shop floor. The three of us kept our own counsel. We had worked out where we would meet if we got the word that our father had died. We knew where we would hide, and we pledged to never again be the victims of funeral arrangements.

Until I went off to college, I shared a room with my bother. "Adam, are you awake?" was one of my questions to the dark. When I said it loudly enough, he always was.

Personal Effects

The images that stick with me are the ghosts of hospital visitations. I've spent a lot of time at the bedside of the dying, and a lot of people looked to me for answers and magic when all I could offer was companionship.

I remember in seminary we were told that a minister entered the hospital room as a representative of a different reality. We were to be a link with other times and places, other people besides the white coats and nursing staff. There was also a spiritual dimension where expectations ran the gamut between hope and voodoo.

The voodoo crowd pleaded the promises of the televangelists. They wanted the "promised" healing, the divine intervention that came through absolute faith. Failing that, they wanted the reminder of guaranteed safe passage into heaven. It's as if saving your own skin is always the highest good, when your skin is the one thing that cannot be saved. Hospitals are never the place to argue. You say the prayer and cross your fingers, not in the anticipation of what God will do, but in the hope that some day they will get it.

There are exceptions. These are the people who have not been afraid of life, so that they are not afraid of death. Don Coyle was one of those people. To this day, I see him sitting on the edge of his hospital bed comforting his daughter who slumped against him in tears. Donna, his namesake, was in junior high at the time. She did not want her father to die. He didn't want to either, but did not seem to have much choice in the matter. Mary, her mother, had taken a walk down the hall, so Donna had been alone with her father when an orderly placed the toe tag on his night stand. This was just after Viet Nam and everyone knew about toe tags and body bags. I have never figured out if the toe tag was delivered by mistake or just someone's idea of efficiency.

As Don comforted his daughter, I realized that I had stumbled into sacred space, a place where the dead comfort the living. If there was any fear in this unassuming man, it was undone by a father's need to care for his child. Twenty-four hours later, I kept a promise to Don by being present when the nurse gave Mary a plastic bag to collect the "personal effects."

Mary told me stories about their years of marriage as I made the rounds by checking the one drawer and the small hanging locker. There was really nothing personal to be found. Don's clothing had been taken home for cleaning. For patients in a hospital, a wallet and identification are rendered useless by unsecured doors and wristbands. The only items were the disposable wash basin and pitcher, a blue kidney-shaped spit cup, and a toothbrush. Of that quartet only the toothbrush seemed at all personal, and that could be tossed easily without regret. I couldn't help but think that the toe tag had become more personal; at least it carried his name!

In reality, the personal effects had been given away the day before, when a father held his daughter and told her that he wasn't afraid.

No Road Home

Good teachers have a way of killing off their students, at least the ones who are paying attention. To this day I can recite the shortlist of those who took part in my homicide, when my all-knowing, assured, adolescent-self came to a sudden end. It was not unwelcome on my part because it felt like the freedom to own my own thoughts and judge between new ideas and the constraints of the past.

Now I sit with a student. As she talks about her term paper her eyes sparkle with energy and I feel a proud complicity in her recent demise. Toward the end, she grows silent.

"I can't go home anymore," she says. I raise an eyebrow and she continues. "My Grandma asks me what I learn in your Religion class and I can't tell her. She thinks that the Bible was written by God, 'Word fo word!'"

I nod; imaging to myself that grandma probably thinks that King James protected it under his pillow while he snuggled with his "Sweet Steenie." I say nothing and she goes on.

"Grandma talks-up my little sister, Shandra. She's pregnant again. Of course Grams doesn't like the father of this one. 'Uses the B-word too much!' she says, and Shandra says I look down on her now that I've been off to college."

Her words make me remember my father's warnings. He had not gone to college and always recited the mantra: "They don't teach you everything in college, so don't get all stuck-up. They don't teach common sense!"

She's a good student, one whose hunger for learning feeds me as well. I give her my short lecture on surviving trips home and enduring house arrest by flying under the radar. I see sadness in her face and maybe some regret over the killing. My mind flits to all the possibilities and I pray that her death survives.

A Flight of Imagination

I remember lying on the floor looking at the ceiling and trading my directional notions of down and up. When I imagined the ceiling as the floor, the entrance to each new room meant straddling a short divider between the two chambers. If the upside down world were flooded, it would be a series of shallow pools like ancient Roman baths. It was about this same time in my early life that I first flew.

Beneath me were the long strands connecting the utility poles, and the top of the pin oak that stood outside my bedroom window. If I came down to alight on one of the telephone poles, I would become frighteningly aware of the height, but rising higher fear vanished beneath the clear view of every roof and clogged gutter on our block.

My dream would always begin with an attempt to fly by force of will. It never worked. Like the nightmares where I could not make leaden feet run faster, I could not will myself into the lightness of the air. If I just relaxed, slipping the grip of gravity opened up the sky.

I am sure that Sigmund would have something to say about the dreams of childhood. I really don't care, but I wouldn't stop him if he wanted to come along. The trip is an adventure worth taking in any company. I would like to learn again the secret of flight that opened my world beyond fear.

About the Author

Born in Youngstown, Ohio and raised in the Cleveland area, Rob Smith has been writing poetry and prose for over forty years. As with many young writers, his creative efforts developed beneath the requirements of career. Nonetheless, he quietly persisted in creating a body of work representative of his imagination. In 2006, he entered his first poetry competition and was awarded the Robert Frost Poetry Award for the poem "Catbird" and published his first novel, *Night Voices*.

Rob now has shifted his use of time by writing full-time, and teaching as an adjunct instructor at both Wright State and Bowling Green State Universities in Ohio. He and his wife, Nancy, now live on the north coast and sail the waters of Lake Erie in an old sloop that they are restoring. Rob holds a bachelor's degree in religion and philosophy from Westminster College (Pa) and master and doctoral degrees from Princeton Theological Seminary. He is editor and publisher of Drinian Press (http://smithwrite.net/drinianpress.html).

Books By
Bottom Dog Press

Our Way of Life $15.00
By Ray McNiee, 978-1-933964-14-0, 132 pages.

Hunger Artist: Childhood in the Suburbs $16.00
By Joanne Jacobson, 978-1-933964-11-9, 132 pages.

Bar Stories $14.00
Edited by Nan Byrne, 14 stories set in the bars of America
978-1-933964-09-6, 176 pages.

d.a.levy & the mimeograph revolution $25.00
Eds. Ingrid Swanberg & Larry Smith, 1-933964-07-3, 276 pages & dvd.

Evensong: Contemporary American Poets on Spirituality $18.00
Eds. Gerry LaFemina & Chad Prevost, 1-933964-01-4, 276 pages.

The Search for the Reason Why: New & Selected Poems $14.00
By Tom Kryss, 0-933087-96-9, 192 pages.

Family Matters: Poems of Our Families $16.00
Eds. Ann Smith and Larry Smith, 0-933087-95-0, 230 pages.

America Zen: A Gathering of Poets $15.00
Eds. Ray McNiece and Larry Smith, 0-933087-91-8, 224 pages.

Street $14.00
Poetry by Jim Daniels, Photographs by Charlee Brodsky
0-933087-93-4, 95 pages.

Bottom Dog Press
PO Box 425 / Huron, OH 44839
http://members.aol.com/Lsmithdog/bottomdog

Books By
Bird Dog Publishing

256 Zones of Gray $14.00
By Rob Smith, 978-1-933-964-16-4, 100 pages.

A Life in Poems $10.00
By William C. Wright, 978-1-933964-15-7, 152 pages.

Second Story Woman: A Memoir of Second Chances $15.00
By Carole Calladine, 978-1-933964-12-6, 226 pages.

Another Life: Collected Poems $14.00
By Allen Frost, 978-1-933964-10-2, 176 pages.

Winter Apples: Poems $14.00
By Paul S. Piper, 978-1-933964-08-9, 88 pages.

Lake Effect: Poems $14.00
By Laura Treacy Bentley, 1-933964-05-7, 108 pages.

Faces and Voices: Tales $14.00
By Larry Smith, 1-933964-04-9, 136 pages.

Depression Days on an Appalachian Farm: Poems $14.00
By Robert L. Tener, 1-933964-03-0, 80 pages.

120 Charles Street, The Village: $15.00
Journals & Other Writings 1949-1950 By Holly Beye,
0-933087-99-3, 240 pages.

Bird Dog Publishing
PO 425/ Huron, OH 4483
http://members.aol.com/Lsmithdog/bottomdog/BirdDogPage.html
A division of Bottom Dog Press, Inc.

LaVergne, TN USA
18 August 2009
155101LV00002B/30/A